IRELAND

IRELA

The Living Landscape

Photographs by Tom Kelly

Text by Peter Somerville-Large

Poetry by Seamus Heaney

Introduction by Tim Pat Coogan

ROBERTS RINEHART PUBLISHERS

ND

For my wife Valerie and to my children Matthew, Emily and Louise.
—Tom Kelly

Published in the United States of America by
Roberts Rinehart Publishers, 121 Second Avenue, Niwot, Colorado 80544

Published in the United Kingdom, Europe, and the Irish Republic by
Roberts Rinehart Publishers, 3 Bayview Terrace, Schull, West Cork

Published in Canada by
Key Porter Books, 70 The Esplanade, Toronto, Ontario M5E 1R2

International Standard Book Number 1-879373-21-1
Library of Congress Catalog Card Number 92-60917
Printed in Hong Kong

Title pages photograph: View from the Rock of Cashel
These pages: "Wherever" (Tom Kelly's description)

CONTENTS

St. Brighid's Holy Well, County Clare

INTRODUCTION

Tom Kelly, Peter Somerville-Large, Seamus Heaney—in one book. Unbidden, Yeats comes to mind:

> Ireland's history in their lineaments trace
> Think where man's glory most begins and ends
> And say my glory was I had such friends.

And then, turning the pages, the Yeatsian motif is reinforced when one comes to Tom Kelly's great bronzed, molten portrait of Ben Bulben. Attempting to describe a photographer's work in words is like learning to swim from a book. The sight of the picture is as essential as the feel of the water. In Kelly's case the images of Ireland that we see through his eyes are the outcome of a conjugation between instinct and professionalism which occurred between the sheets of artistry; of twenty years of the sort of painstaking research that is more associated with the scientist in the laboratory than the photographer in the field. Waiting on a western coast for three days to catch the exact light at the precise moment that the wave breaks to the best advantage. Loitering by the Liffey until the familiar Guiness boat is magically transformed by mist and an offering of swans into an icon of nostalgia. No one but an Irish photographer could know when to go and where to see that peak most advantageously gleam with snow, this range lower into dusk, or catch a favourite island dreaming in the moonlight.

It is fitting that this lensman poet of place should have his work adorned by singers of race and place of the stature of Seamus Heaney and Peter Somerville-Large. Heaney, whose soft-voiced readings of poems inspired by such essentially Irish phenomena as a bog or a pilgrimage island have hushed into reverential awe audiences in temples of sophistication from Harvard to Oxford, is an artist who has indeed called the Muses home. In the words of Yeats, whose mantle, many feel, has fallen on Heaney's shoulders:

> Though the great song return no more
> There's keen delight in what we have
> The rattle of pebble on the shore
> Under the receding wave.

But along with delight there can also be melancholia. The effect of bogs and fogs entertwine sometimes with a poverty of mind and pocket that is the product of two forms of colonialism, those emanating from London and Rome. These erstwhile dependencies interact with the short-sighted avarice of generations that used Irish independence as a means of emulating the exploiters, but with less style. No writer in Ireland has more entitlement to remind us of these things than Peter Somerville-Large. His fidelity to his subject is such that, in the month of January, he once walked through Ireland from Bantry bay to County Leitrim. He was trying to recreate for himself some sense of the heroism and the horror that marked the retreat of Sullivan Beare and his followers. He writes of his footsore odyssey:

> Day after day rain bathed the landscape in a grey cloud; the fields
> were sodden and silent with the occasional sound of cattle coughing.
> Black birds burst out of leafless trees covered in ivy…

However, along with his reminders of the dark, he illuminates the pleasant things also. The old beliefs, the glorious landscapes, the exuberance of country life. He reminds us that war-torn Northern Ireland is a place of beauty also. He tells us how the country is changing and warns of the hidden costs of progress. Rightly so. Ireland after all disgraced itself by trampling on the dreams of Monet and Schumann, the fathers of the European Community, when the twenty-six counties entered the EEC. Kathleen Ni Houlihan embarked not on a race toward the golden dawn of opportunity for Irish agriculture, then the country's most important single industry, but on a Gaderene rush into intervention and its attendant scandals. Both landscape and cities have suffered from despoilation by the hard-faced men who did well out of peace:

> …uncontrolled ribbon development, a bungalow built beside a beauty
> spot, hedges torn up, heather-covered mountains smothered in sombre fir trees,
> pollution of our lakes, Georgian buildings gone to ruin and all the signs of
> destruction.

Somerville-Large sounds the tocsin, not out of a spirit of begrudgery (all three contributors to this book are far above that familiar Irish failing), but to remind us of what the Irish and the world stand to lose from the destruction of Ireland's environmental treasure trove. Tom Kelly's pictures are literally a glowing testament to their worth and this book will be a lasting testimonial to the talents of both its publisher and contributors.

Tim Pat Coogan

AN IRISH MOSAIC

Consider a number of random images of Ireland:

In the first a bull grazes in a field in County Limerick above a horseshoe-shaped lake, where once every seven years the magician Earl of Desmond rides over the waters on his silver-shod shoes. Castles, crannogs, a line of dolmens, reeds, and the bright green of limestone pasture are part of the landscape of Lough Gur; so is the little farmhouse where Sissy O'Brien spent her childhood, details of which she related in old age to Mary Carbury.

We ... had a store of country knowledge. We knew about butter making, candle making, spinning and weaving, how sheep were washed and sheared, and the way pigs have rings set in their snouts, how eels are caught and fairies exorcised from dairies.

Another place: the ridge of Slieve na Calliagh above Oldcastle in County Meath commanding wide-ranging views of lakes, hills, and lush farmland. At its foot near a small lake, Loughcrew, are scattered huge pieces of stone and masonry, all that remains of a Palladian house that stood on land that once belonged to the Plunkett family, one of whose illustrious members was Blessed Oliver, archbishop of Armagh, executed at Tyburn. By contrast, the summit is scattered with tumuli, cairns, a ring fort, a pillarstone, and stones carved with ancient patterns, which together form part of an extensive neolithic cemetery.

An island in Roaring Water bay has a ruined church dedicated to a Celtic saint standing on a cliff's edge; coffins can be made out in the cliff face like a chest of drawers. The island is empty except for wrens, robins, stonechats, larks, and seabirds. A few traces remain of the people who once lived there: gable ends, stone walls, nettles, and grass-quilted potato fields. In spring, daffodils can be seen blooming bravely round the ruins.

Here are three ancient examples of scenery blended by tradition, mystery, and melancholy. History intrudes, whether in the form of magic and legend contrasted with idealized pastoral custom, prehistory combined with conquest, or a time that is within living memory when poverty has destroyed an island community. Elsewhere, whether in the boggy wastes of Mayo, the deserted Blasket islands, the hills of Donegal, the Glens of Antrim, or a thousand other places, the past dominates. The poignancy that pervades the Irish landscape has to do not only with the calamities of history but also with age.

Geologically, Ireland is ancient. The land surface is older than that of most other European countries. Dramatic changes of climate, the passing of grilling deserts of New Red sandstone, and the flooding and retreating of coral and tropical seas are among the geological episodes that have formed the land. Most recently, the Ice Age left its signature with its U-shaped valleys and drumlins. The boulders on the slopes of the Scalp outside Dublin were deposited by ice; the quartzite peaks of the Sugarloaves—as distinctive to Wicklow as Mount Fujiama is to Japan—protruded over the ice sheet fifteen thousand years ago. The long graceful shapes of the esker ridges that stretch across the midlands, which have been compared to lines of fish, torpedoes, and even racing cars, have been called "dead" landforms because the agency that created the ice is no longer present.

Inland, the central plain is ribbed with ranges of hills whose modest peaks manage to impose a scale upon the landscape at variance with their height. Single mountains standing alone—such as Brandon in West Kerry, the silvery quartz beacon of Errigal; Mount Gabriel above Roaring Water bay, where a slipping bog has revealed extensive prehistoric copper mines; and Slievenamon, the Hill of the Women—are focuses for legend. The effect of humidity or cold and changing light patterns enhances the effect of size. The uplands on the coast, particularly the west coast, often rise sheer from the sea, as do the Cliffs of Moher in County Clare and the great height of Slieve League in Donegal. The peaks of the twelve Bens that ruffle the skyline of Connemara, the shadowy outline of the Mournes seen from Dublin far in the northern distance, and the line of the Slieve Miskish above Bantry bay each suggest the presence of Celtic gods. Mountain grandeur reaches an imposing splendour with the jagged Macgillicuddy Reeks in Kerry, although Carrantuohill, the highest mountain in Ireland, is a mere 3414 feet high. The Galtees and Knockmealdowns run parallel through Tipperary and north Cork; eastwards Waterford is dominated by

the Comeraghs. History and legend have their place among the little ranges—wrinkles on the flat land—such as the Slieve Blooms, the Ballyhoura hills that mark the west end of the Galtee range, the Curlieus where the last great Irish battle before Kinsale was fought and won, and the Bricklieves, with their stepped sides and limestone cover.

Brian Merriman's view of the hills of Clare will do for all the hills of Ireland:

> *Taitneamhach aoibhinn suíomh na sléibhte*
> *ag bagairt a gcinn thar droim a chéile.*

> The sweet and delightful set of the mountains
> looming their heads up over each other.

Rivers lace the central plain and cut through the mountains; Slaney, Bride, Lee, Suir, Aherlow, Nore, Liffey, the great Boyne, the Bann, the Lagan, and a hundred others carry their history from mountain source to sea. Some are eel-thin, their waves tea-coloured; others such as the Barrow and the Blackwater are navigable for many miles. The Shannon, the longest river in the British Isles, moves slowly across the central lowland through its lakes before descending at its tidewater above Limerick and emerging at the drowned valley that is its estuary.

"Only for my short Brittas bed made's as snug as it smells it's out I'd lep and off with me to the slobs della Tolka or the plage au Clontarf to feale the gay aire of my salt troublin bay and the race of the saywint up me ambushrue." James Joyce's unusual view of geography gives a stretch of the old river that leads into Dublin and bursts out into the bay. Near its headwaters the Liffey's curious meanderings—largely submerged by the Blessington reservoir—were determined by geographical conditions that pertained to preglacial times.

Lakes vary from "pools among the rushes that scarce could bathe a star," to the overpraised (perhaps) beauties of Killarney, to the scores that lie in the pockmarked landscape of Leitrim, to those strung like beads on a necklace along the Shannon and the Erne, to the huge flat circle of Lough Neagh. The boglands of the central plain, the rich limestone of the lowlands, the bleak karst pavements of the Burren, granite-dominated Wicklow, Kerry sandstone, the remains of volcanic activity around Lough Gur, and the effects of the sea's buffeting, which has carved out great fiords such as Bantry bay and the Kenmare river, help to impose an immense variation of landscape on a tiny island whose total area is about that of the state of Pennsylvania.

Climate imposes its own variety: the clouds; the clear heaven; and the restless effects of rain, fleeting sunshine, and shifting light. The shape of the landscape and the vegetation owes much to the wind. The island's position at the end of Europe beside the Atlantic seaboard brings a constant wash of moisture-laden westerly winds. Wind and rain are constant sources of attrition, particularly in the west, where a precipitation of more than sixty inches is average.

I am still surprised to find even in an area I think I know well some unexpected corner … a hidden lake or boreen, an ancient church or ivy-covered ruin, a new view of a mountain range, or magical hawthorn standing alone in a field. The genial stranger, John Betjeman, hymned Ireland's variety.

> Lush Kildare of scented meadow,
> Roscommon thin in ash-tree shadow
> And Westmeath the lake reflected,
> Spreading Leix the hill-protected
> Kneeling all in silver haze.
>
> Stony seaboard, far and foreign
> Stony hills poured over space,
> Stony outcrop of the Burren,
> Stones in every fertile place.

Like so many who sing Ireland's praises, Betjeman ignored Northern Ireland. Betjeman's poem predates the recent troubles, but for many of us the border has meant a rejection of a large part of our island. Television news has played its part; when we think of the landscape of the north it is usually a country lane in the border area where something evil has just happened. The northern rural scene is largely unexplored: the Mourne mountains, the Lough Erne waterways, and the extraordinary, diverse coastline. A coastal journey from Lough Foyle in Derry eastwards toward Magilligan strand, the largest in Ireland, will lead the traveller on to the Gothic drama of Dunluce castle, Rathlin island, the amazing Giants causeway, Fairhead (from where Scotland seems only a step away across the water) and the surprising beauty of the Glens of Antrim.

The variety of Irish landscape is not matched by any richness in fauna and flora. Over hundreds of thousands of years of geological change, animal species have diminished. I remember as a child visiting that ark of bygone creation, the National History Museum in Dublin. Glass-covered trays of ancient bones provided evidence of prehistoric species that once inhabited Ireland: a woolly mammoth's tusk, the tooth of a sabre-tooth tiger, a splinter of bone from a bear that lived in County Cork, or the remains of wolves, a species that was hunted out by the end of the seventeenth century.

Another creature that became extinct within living memory was the white-tailed eagle that inhabited the high mountains of the west coast until it was destroyed as an unwanted predator. Arthur Fox saw one of the last at Glenveigh at the beginning of the twentieth century: "A male bird just emerged from the moulting season and in fine plumage, deeply brown with his tail slightly white-barred … while his golden head and breast shone vividly in the lustrous light." All the eagles have gone now; there is a stuffed white-tailed specimen in the museum. Perhaps recent attempts to reintroduce the king of birds into Ireland may succeed.

Grandest of all of Ireland's animals was the Irish giant elk, whose majestic antlers measured ten feet or more. They were for show rather than combat; the stag would discourage rivals by the size of his antlers. These animals strutted about the hills until they died, crashing into a bog under a mad weight. Herds of them grazed the heather on Glencullen outside Dublin. At nearby Ballybetagh bog the remains of more than thirty giant elk were found a half century ago by the scientist Dr. Stokes, who prodded the oozy brown surface with a pole to discover the elk bones.

Today we must be content with something less spectacular in the way of animals. There are less than half the amount of native species in Ireland than in England. We have no weasels or moles here. There are only two amphibians, the frog and the newt. The dearth of reptiles, whether or not by the hand of St. Patrick, has left us with just one species, the lizard, which is rare enough for his appearance to have the impact of that of a little dragon. Reptiles persist in folklore, lingering as monsters in the depths of many lakes. There is also a shortfall in the number of bird species: In Ireland 354 varieties of avians can be found as against more than 400 in England.

It is the same with plants. The Ice Age destroyed much vegetation so that plant life had to begin again and reestablish itself. It was immensely restricted when the land bridge that joined Ireland to England was severed. The range of habitats is also limited, and as a result there are just over nine hundred species of flowering plants in Ireland, one-third less than in Britain.

In the last century many changes have occurred in the other direction, and Ireland has been enriched by a number of plant introductions that have spectacularly affected the countryside. Fuchsia and montbretia brighten summer hedgerows. The buddleia, or butterfly plant, has adapted to waste places; so has red valerian, originally from Asia Minor and once an Elizabethan garden plant. The rhododendron, killed off in Ireland by the cold of the Ice Age more than thirty thousand years ago, left pollen to be detected in samples taken from acid bogs. Reintroduced as a garden exotic from the Himalayas, rhododendron has adapted to its old home so that now it is a showy, rampant weed. The coarse, almost reptilian, dark-green gunnera creeps round the west, particularly on Achill island. Balsam chokes the riverbanks, and the giant hogweed claims boggy ground, looking like triffids. The wet infertile soils of western Ireland—the uplands and stretches of blanket bog—are widely cultivated with plantations of fir trees, whose dour green ranks furring the bleak country are the subject of much controversy.

Modern agricultural practises, such as the elimination of hedges, threaten the symmetry of the landscape. The old turnip crops so beloved by Arthur Young have been largely replaced by currently desirable crops such as rape and sugar beet. There are other manifestations of ugliness, both ancient and modern: indiscriminate construction, rubbish, neglect, damp, nettles, and "the two-headed briar." But beauty is still here for us to find and for the photographer to stalk, waiting for a particular cloud formation, a rainbow, the effect of distilled light, the highest point of foam on the waves beating on rocks, or other moments when the camera can capture miracles of nature. The poet can also record a moment for us, so that today we can find the same joy in the countryside as did Bryan Merriman, stepping out one early summer morning three hundred years ago:

> *Do ghealfadh an croí bheadh críon le cianta,*
> *caite gan bhrí, nó líonta de phianta.*

> It would brighten a heart worn out with time
> or spent, or faint, or filled with pain…
> to gaze for a while across the woods

at the shoals of ducks on the cloudless bay
and a swan between them, sailing with them,
at fishes jumping on high for joy,
the flash of a stripe-bellied glittering perch,
the hue of the lake, the blue of the waves
heavy and strong as they rumble in.
Translated by Séan Ó Tuama
and Thomas Kinsella

Climate and geological history have played their part in shaping the landscape, but much of what we see and appreciate as beautiful is human-made. The Ireland of forest and bog has been changing from the moment prehistoric humans first climbed into skin boats and sailed over from England and Scotland. The first inhabitants of Ireland were hunters and shell gatherers whose kitchen middens are still to be found on the Antrim coast. The neolithic farmers who followed them cleared the forest and built houses whose remains include a hearth and refuse pit. They became farmers and herdsmen; their wealth was cattle and corn, and so it would remain for Irish farmers for thousands of years. In a country where the vast majority of people have made their living from agriculture, it is unsurprising that the abiding passion for so many country people has been a hunger for land.

The statistics of land ownership are dramatic. From a small minority of three percent of big landlords who virtually owned Ireland as a result of the various Land Acts, to the eclipse of the landlord class and the consequences of independence, (in little more than a century) land ownership has been totally transformed. The elimination of the landlord, whose symbol of domination was the stone wall, has had its effect on landscape—not always beneficial. Huge estates were broken up and divided, trees were felled, and old houses, many of them buildings of great architectural beauty, were burned or torn down.

Today Ireland is a nation of small farmers with an average farm of less than a hundred acres. But the drastic changes of agriculture during the 1970s and 1980s under the auspices of the European Community have meant that many of these smaller uneconomic farms are unable to survive, and poverty persists. Even in the 1990s almost ninety-seven percent of Ireland's landmass, virtually unaffected by the Industrial Revolution, remains rural. The price for this has been the persistence of poverty and emigration.

There is seldom a vista even among the bleakest mountains or across a stretch of bog where a ruin or a human-made monument does not have a place in the scenery. Ring forts, megalithic tombs, churches, high crosses, castles, and great houses all contribute to the image of Ireland, helping to impart a particular atmosphere that can only be defined as romantic. One or two emotional observers have labelled such views incorporating some human-made piece of architecture as "heartbreaking." The dank climate can cloak the most recent ruin with the appearance of antiquity, as festoons of ivy cover the walls of an abandoned Victorian mill, a roofless Protestant church, or the broken walls of an estate. The ruins most satisfying to the romantic spirit are not those where money is paid and a guided tour is offered. The true pleasure of ruins is to be found in the chamber tomb hidden in bracken on a hillside, in a castle standing unnoticed in a field surrounded by barbed wire, or in the remains of a fish palace where pilchards were cured. Nancy Mitford, visiting the Blackwater valley thirty years ago caught the mood.

The green deserted fields lying beneath blue deserted mountains; the windowless mills dripping with creepers; the towers for captive princesses ... the endless walls surrounding ghostly demesnes; the roofless churches ... make a melancholy but enchanted impression.

Other observers have also romanticized the thatched cottage, whose mud walls and weeping were redolent of poverty rather than beauty. It is well that the thatched cottage has almost vanished. And yet the sight of a survivor in Connemara or Donegal—the straw roof tied down with stones—still evokes a view of rural life that for decades was a part of politics. Eamon De Valera's chaste and comely maidens and his exhortation of frugality and hard work blessed by the church contributed to a desire to express in nationalistic rhetoric a vision of an idealized rural past. Fuelled by such different elements as the Blasket Island literature, national politics, folk memory of past tyranny, and the Gaelic revival, this ideal persists in the face of modern political and rural change. It pervades the landscape, perhaps because to some extent it is still here or has only recently departed. "With seven children in the family, we were reared as free as birds, growing up in a world of simplicity untouched by outside influences. Our farm was our world and nature as an educator gave free reign to our imaginations."

Anyone over fifty remembers with nostalgia the era of oil lamps, horses rather than tractors, homemade butter and salted bacon, the cow milked by hand, and the cream and milk in the dairy. Now the days of the horse and cart, the winnowing machine, the furze machine, and the threshing machine are over. The countryside has been changed by the capital invested in it as the mart and the factory, the pig unit, the battery shed, and the Credit Corporation take over the running of the farm. "Farming is a very good business now," an old man told me. "In the old days it wouldn't raise cats." It is right that the poverty that gave an edge to the old rural life is softened. But the past has moulded the present, and it is permissible to allow history, folk memory, and legend to play their part in considering the landscape season by season.

SPRING
an t earrach

Traditionally, spring begins on St. Brighid's Day, February the first, and lasts until May Day, but in fact it stretches from the first snowdrop in mid-January to mid-May, when oak and ash have completed their race to bring out late-budding leaves.

Brighid was a Celtic goddess of poetry and learning; the little cowherd who was her Christian namesake was born in the sixth century and became patroness of Ireland. Her feast day coincided with the pagan festival Imbolg, the first day of spring, and the advent of spring ploughing. Making crooked crosses from rushes and hanging them in the home and byre is a tradition that lingers, although children no longer go scraping hoar frost from the fields as a cure for headache. In valleys around Killarney I have seen groups of mummers who still wander from house to house carrying the Biddy, or Brideog, a pink doll wearing a mitre—adorned with a rush cross.

After her feast the saint expected the weather to improve:

> Every second day fine
> From my day onward
> and half of my day...

But spring is gradual and prolonged. The early signs of its approach—the spread of blackthorn blossom in the hedges, the birdsong, and the lengthening of days—cannot prevent the changes from seeming painfully slow. The progress of the yellow flower is one signal: first coltsfoot and then the ubiquitous dandelion. Marsh marigold makes a brilliant dash of colour in wet spring meadows. The celandine will bloom in January a little later than the snowdrop, whose inner petals form an inverted bell containing a puff of trapped air that is warmer than surrounding frost, heated for early bees to find. But bees are scarce in January, and the reproductive powers of the snowdrop, which does not stray outside the garden or churchyard, have proven less successful than the adaptable celandine.

Primrose is from the medieval Latin, *prima rosa*, the first rose of the year. In Ireland it is the samhaircín, the May flower, although the time of its flowering can begin in February in the southwest of the country and linger far into summer; I have found primroses blooming on Omey island on the fourth of July.

Nowadays ploughing starts in October and continues right into spring. The tractor moving the plough that breaks the first furrow has long succeeded the horse; the tractor pulls two or three ploughs, which dig seven or eight inches turning over the furrows, burying straw and weeds, and reversing the sod. Old men recall the skill of ploughing with horses and the effort of keeping the furrow straight—a crooked furrow would earn the scorn of every man in the townland. The seagulls followed so closely that they could be hit with the reins. "Today they can only plough and harrow sitting on their backsides up on the tractor."

> Black wings and white in the hollow
> Follow the track of the team,
> While the sun from the noon declining
> Is shining on toil-wet brows.
> Birds of the mountain and sea-birds
> Circle and swoop and scream,
> Searching for spoils of the furrow
> Where slowly the ploughman ploughs.
> James H. Cousins

St. Patrick's feast may be as chilled as St. Brighid's. On many a Patrick's Day a cold wind blows across newly ploughed fields trellised with snow. Frogspawn appears in stagnant water; a Gaelic name for frog was *leiprachan an chlaí,* the leprechaun of the ditch. In this glum season for celebration, Christian and Celtic festival are linked once again, as the legends of the enigmatic Christian saint blend with the spring equinox. St. Patrick's Day, when lambing is well advanced and crops are sown, is traditionally the last day for foxhounds and beagles to be out: "I tore my old britches gone over the ditches on St. Patrick's Day in the morning."

This is the day for gathering shamrock—the little plant with a pedigree almost as mysterious as St. Patrick's but most often identified as trifolium dubium, the lesser yellow trefoil. Once a charm against sorcery and witches, the shamrock gained new symbolism when St. Patrick ingeniously used it to explain the Trinity. It must be found accidentally—as small boys we searched for it on that cold mid-March morning before pinning it on our jackets.

On St. Patrick's Day my elderly aunt used to travel to Tara and climb up to the ancient royal site with her harp. The hill of Tara with its great view of the plains of Meath offers one more sweep of history. The lumps and bumps that remain of past glories lie beside a little nineteenth-century First Fruits Protestant Church set in trees, containing an ancient *sheila-na-gig,* one of the obscene little fertility symbols which, like round towers, used to embarrass antiquarians. Near the Mound of the Hostages and the Royal Enclosure my aunt sat and plucked Moore's melodies and robust hymns to St. Patrick.

> No more to chiefs and ladies bright
> The harp of Tara swells...

Traditionally the first nine days of April were called "the borrowed days":

> Three days for fleecing the blackbird
> Three days of punishment for the stone-chat
> And three days for the grey cow...

The floors of woodlands are covered with anemones and bluebells, and the hillsides begin to carry the gold and clove scent of furze. "The hedges on the way to St. Patrick's well were full of primroses," Sissy O'Brien described one Easter Sunday. "Lamb's tails dangled from the hazel boughs, sending tiny puffs of pollen in the sunshine; from the sky fell the song of larks." On Easter day children were warned not to look directly at the sun but only at its reflection in a tub of clear water. Old people remember gathering young nettles and eating them like spinach as a spring tonic.

On the mountainside the larch puts out its early brilliant green nettles, followed by the delicate foliage of birch and rowan. Young leaves of horse chestnut trees unfold and stiffen; by May they will support the striking "candles" of white flowers. The trees and shrubs dominating the countryside where the sitka has not taken over are mainly old native species such as oak, mountain ash, hawthorn, birch, holly, willow, elder, and blackthorn.

The ancient forests were threatened from the time that neolithic humans first started ring-barking trees to clear space for agriculture. By the Middle Ages laws were passed discouraging with fines the felling of trees, particularly "noble trees" such as oak, yew, and hazel. Oak was an essential of carpentry and its bark was used in tanning, and acorns provided food for swine. But well-grown oaks were already becoming scarce. Yew trees, once prized by master carpenters, are rare in the wild and are now mainly confined to churchyard and demesne. The yew tree was sacred, its wood used for bishops' croziers and book shrines. Hazel is the great survivor, ready to spread across abandoned land; once it was valued for its nuts, an important item in the medieval diet, and for its coppiced stems, which were used in wattle work.

The forest was the focus of legends, according to which the blessed madman Suibne roamed the woodlands and lived in the treetops. It also was a refuge for hermits seeking solitude. St. Kevin, praying quietly in the forests of Glendalough, attracted a thrush, which built a nest in his hands and raised fledglings. The blessed Kieran of Sagir had a wild boar, a badger, and a fox as disciples. Other hermits contemplated the woodland birds and composed poetry to them; it was the birds, according to legend, that first welcomed St. Patrick to Ireland.

> A flock of birds bright as the sun,
> Each clothed in a hundred feathers
> Together they sing clearly
> A hundred songs for every feather.

The destruction of the old native woods gathered pace after the Elizabethan conquest; a market for charcoal and a wish to reduce cover for robbers, rebels, and rapparees encouraged a massive programme of tree felling. Alas, the felling of ancient forests has continued until the present day; in the 1980s a great stand of trees was destroyed near Shillelagh, whose name was given to a celebrated oak weapon. But a few remnants of old Irish forest still can be seen, particularly at Glengarriff and Killarney, at Killeagh in East Cork, and in pockets of the Wicklow hills, where the oaks struggle for survival with the returned exile, the rhododendron.

The spring birds start to fly in. From the cliffs of Cape Clear on the migratory route south of West Cork the watcher can count hundreds of fulmars, shearwaters, kittiwakes, and other seabirds passing on their way to their nesting sites. On land the cuckoo arrives, which, like the corncrake, has grown rare. The swallow, having set out from its winter quarters in East Africa, reaches Ireland well before the swift. Some people date the arrival of the swift, early in May, as the beginning of summer. Of the four hundred or so birds to be seen in Ireland, only a hundred or so are resident, remaining here all the year. Resident or summer visitor, however, spring is their time. All over woodlands and open country clockwork chatter is heard: the scratch and squeak of stonechat, the whirr of angry wren, the jingle of lark, and the sounds of other nesting birds.

The climate of Ireland in spring is expressed in its clouds. The wide skies give a continuous restless display of high cirrus; towering cumulus; the aerial cauliflower, cirro-stratus; nimbo-stratus, and the cumulo-nimbus capillatus, a pompous term for a storm cloud. Storm clouds can go through two development phases, bald (calvus) and then hairy (capillatus)—terms that describe their initial state and final conformation. From Torca cottage in Dalkey, outside Dublin, the young George Bernard Shaw looked out over "the two great bays between Howth and Bray Head" and remembered for the rest of his life the "canopied skies such as I have never seen elsewhere in the world."

Rain in spring is as unpredictable and prolonged as in any other period of the year. The geologist Frank Mitchell writes that there is no such thing as climate in Ireland, but only an irregular sequence of different weather patterns, with the emphasis on frontal systems bringing wind and rain. The folklorist E. Estyn Evans mused:

One wonders why in the beginning men chose to live in this far-off rain-soaked land. Would they have stayed on reaching these shores from sunnier parts, if they could have heard a long-range forecast? It will be wet almost everywhere, but a few sunny intervals may occur from time to time.

summer
an samhradh

Delightful is the season's splendour
Rough winter has gone
Every fruitful wood shines white
A joyous peace in summer.

If the rural ideal often disguised a life of slavery and hard work, the coming of summer, with its longer days and time for leisure, could only be a blessing. "We welcomed it and the freedom it brought from the shackles of winter," wrote Alice Taylor, remembering her Cork childhood in the 1940s.

May Day coincided with Beltane, the Celtic feast, a time for lighting fires on the hills, decorating the May bush, and collecting yellow flowers. The sun was supposed to rise extra early on May Day, which was a day for witchcraft and magic spells when witches and fairies were active. Milk and butter were liable to be stolen or bewitched; the surest protection was

Atlantic coast

provided by the rowan tree. "Old pishogues," an old man recently told me, remembering the custom of his youth, when stables were sprinkled with holy water and girls looked for snails and collected May dew, while men refrained from smoking as they entered the house. They still decorate doorways with a sprig of green in the town where I live.

Summer brings festivals, regattas, feis, patterns, processions, pilgrimages, Puck Fair, flat racing, and the mounting tension of Gaelic games culminating with the hurling and football finals in September. There also are the new festivals for the tourists, summer schools and golf tournaments.

Summer! Summer! The milk of the heifers
And ourselves brought the summer with us,
the yellow summer; and the white daisy,
And ourselves brought the summer with us.

The yellow of summer, heralded by buttercup, is succeeded by gorse, which is at its most brilliant in early May. Furze flowers are almost constant, although the saying that kissing is out of season when furze is out of flower cheats, as the two species—the clove-scented *Ulex europeus* and the summer-blooming *Ulex gallii*—spread the yellow flowers over most of the year. Furze has lost its uses as winter cattle feed crushed with wooden mauls and even as a place to dry clothes. In medieval times furze was planted on the boundary of fields to provide ready fuel. Today it is regarded as a nuisance to be burned early in the year to make room for sheep fodder.

The brimstone of the rape harvest is a recent addition to summer's yellow. In late summer the poisonous ragweed, the farmer's peril, whose stiff stalks provided a mount for witches to ride through the skies, will dominate neglected pastures. The festival passage can also be marked by the progress of the white flower—rowan, hawthorn, and elder, all associated with magic. Rowan, which will grow at a higher altitude than any other tree, is the tree for protection. Planted in a graveyard, it will keep the dead from rising. Lone hawthorn trees where fairies meet are still left to themselves; cut the lone thorn and it may bleed or scream. It is believed that Judas Iscariot hanged himself on the elder. The timber of elder may not be burned lest you see the devil in the fire or used in the making of boats, which will capsize. Nor is it safe to make elder into a cradle because the child will be stolen by fairies.

Although the arum growing so easily in gardens in the west is named the Easter lily, it blooms best in May. In woodlands the wild garlic will succeed the bluebell. On sea cliffs and rocky shores, thrift, or sea pink, blossoms thickly from its blue-green cushion. Many of Mary's flowers come into bloom. The name *Mary* features constantly in the names of flowers. Creeping cinquefoil is *cuig mhear Mhuire*, Mary's five fingers. St. John's wort is *allas Mhuire*, Mary's perspiration, and both foxgloves and the white spikes of pennywort that grow on walls are known as Mary's candles.

Kerry and the extreme west of County Cork are the locations for unusual Lusitanian plants such as the golden clumps of Irish spurge, giant butterwort the size of Parma violets, and St. Patrick's cabbage, whose green rosettes and lacy pink flowers seek rocks and shade. But the early summer reaches its most dramatic expression in the limestone wilderness of the Burren in late May. The Burren is the place for megalithic tombs standing on flat, tinkling limestone rock, hazel woods, hawthorn, ancient castles, turloughs (hollows filled with lakes at times and completely dry at others), and the severed heads around the doorway of Dysert O'Dea. The dominant mountain, Mullagh More, ascends in a helix like Mount Purgatory. The distinctive artic-alpine flora includes saxifrage; a rare orchid, *Neotinea intacta*; cranesbill; ice blue gentians; and mountain avens, an uncommon arctic-alpine plant with white starred flowers and leaves like miniature oak leaves.

The Irish cattle industry is based on dairy farming, with a summer milk production ending in September or October. Traditionally farmers would rub cows' udders with buttercups on May Day. It is hardly surprising that milk has always been a favourite nourishment among the Irish, "generally being the greatest lovers of milk I ever saw," according to a seventeenth-century observer, "which they eat and drink about twenty several sorts of ways, and what is the strangest, love it best when sourest."

Modern cattle are subject to fashion; the old nineteenth-century shorthorn, which continued in popularity up to the first half of this century, is never seen today. An old farmer told me how, at the fairs, "I would look for a heifer with two hips standing up in front of the tail, and a good round rib not falling off the backbone at all." Among dairy cattle the shorthorn gave way to the black-and-white Freisan, whereas the Herefords and Hereford crosses, which dominated the beef herds, are replaced by big brown and grey Continental breeds such as the Simenthal and Limousin.

The old tough little cows and bulls that made up the native herd, the beasts of legend, and cattle drivers linger intermittently. My mother kept a herd of small black Kerry cows, one of the few surviving breeds of medieval cattle. They gave rich milk, which was turned into strong, homemade butter and stored in crocks. I always associated these cows with the beginning of summer, when they were turned out to graze on the bog meadow.

With summer rain bringing a plentiful supply of pasture, the old custom of "booleying" was practised, when cattle were brought up to the higher slopes of the mountain and their drovers lodged in "booley huts"—stone buildings whose scattered remains can still be found. Singing and dancing enlivened the long summer evenings, a break from the drudgery of chores on the lowland farms. The acrid modern word for booleying is transhumance. Today, sheep and fir trees have taken over the rocky slopes where cattle once grazed.

Haymaking is losing its place in farm economy as the regular cropping of silage takes over and winter fodder is thrown about the fields in shining plastic rolls. In fact the hay harvest only assumed importance in medieval times; it did not play a significant part in the traditional Gaelic system of farming until changes took place in agrarian practises. In the north of Ireland the first hay cutting is fixed to coincide with the Orange Festival on the twelfth of July. The tedious and beautiful rhythms of scything, drying, and stacking are ceasing to be part of the farming year; so are the miseries of wet summers when the hay was uncut by late August or lay rotting and black on the ground. "We only grow a bit for the calves," a farmer told me recently. "In the old days you'd be hanging around for the stuff the whole bloody summer."

Below the mountains the tracts of bog are diminishing. If we are to believe the statistics, one-seventh of Ireland is covered in bog. Once bogs not only skirted the mountains but also covered much of the midlands in their wet embrace. Although bogs provided the ingredients for cooking and warmth, their extent made them regarded as hostile wastes. In some places they seemed to stretch forever. The botanist Lloyd Praeger described how "from Mallarney you may walk for thirty miles to the giant cliffs of north Mayo, you may never leave the heather save that twice you cross a road, fenceless, winding like a narrow white ribbon through the endless brown bog."

Bogs are preservatives; "a bog acts as a passive receiver and storer of information," notes the naturalist David Bellamy, "like a vast sheet of blotting paper which soaks up any pollen, grains and spores that blow its way and fall upon its surface." Bogs preserve not only seeds, insects, and bleached remains of early forests, but also traces of humans. A neolithic farm uncovered under a thick coating of bogland in May wooden methars for storing bog butter, and treasure, such as gold torcs, bracelets, and other ornaments that may be concealed under its dark brown cover. One recent and spectacular find was the Derrynaflann hoard, dug up in Tipperary, a ninth-century paten and strainer and a chalice that rivals the Ardagh chalice for intricate workmanship. Very occasionally clothes will be found that dressed a corpse, the corpse itself having melted away under the influence of bogwater. One example in the National Museum in Dublin is a coat with three ties, a balaclava helmet, felt boots (in one of which was found a toenail, all that was left of its owner), and a shroud. Discovered in 1946 near Hollyford, County Tipperary, these poignant garments were locally believed to belong to a follower of O'Sullivan Beare who perished during the epic march in 1601.

Fifty years ago the raised bogs of the midlands were still largely as nature had made them, and cutting turf was a cottage industry as much a part of the farming year as dairying. Even today on the bogs of Connemara and Mayo, people are winning turf by hand, opening up the bank for the first cutting in May after the bogland has dried. There used to be something deeply satisfying in digging out the black layers of turf embedded under the sphagnum moss. A week's work by a family would provide fuel for a year. After cutting came the drying process, when through the summer the turves were footed and stacked, catching the drying winds; *turnsfoot, castles, ickles, lumps*, and *clamps* were some of the names given to turf stacks. Smoke from the turf fire is the most aromatic and welcoming scent for the returning wanderer.

In the past a few brave and generally misguided attempts were made to develop bogs, like Richard Pochrich's wild scheme in the eighteenth century for turning them into quagmires for raising ducks and geese or alternatively for planting them with vines. The state body, Bord na Mona, began a systematic cutting of bog in 1946; for years Ireland ranked second only to the U.S.S.R. in the production of mechanized turf. But now that turf is exhausted and the great cooling towers that hang over a devastated landscape may become as extinct as the bogland they destroyed.

Like turf, wrack (or seaweed), is a resource there for the taking—to be cut, loaded into boats, and spread on wrack walls to dry. Many species of seaweed grow around the Irish coast. Knob wrack was considered equal to meadow hay, dulaman was chewed or eaten with potatoes, carragheen was made into a jelly or a hot drink, and even the stems or sea-rods were a rich source of iodine. Unlike turf, wrack is self-sufficient, replacing itself through a natural cycle every four years.

I remember the cartloads of wrack spread out in small Kerry fields and later a rich harvest of vegetables. As a boy I knew the joys of summer living on a small island in the Kenmare river: neap tides; long days when land and sea became diffused in haze; the sight of seals, otters, dolphins, and herons; fishing for mackerel in small boats, gathering mussels, and sea urchins—*grainnéog na farraige*—the hedgehog of the sea.

Both turf and seaweed were essential to the island life where a remarkable community turned their experiences into literature. One high narrow island, the Great Blasket, harboured a small group of hardy islanders, three of whom—Tomás ÓCrohan, Peig Sayers, and Maurice O'Sullivan—produced classic accounts of their hardships and joys, highlighting the lonely, often grim, often rewarding lifestyle of a struggling yet self-sufficient community. The Blasket islanders left their homes forty years ago; one of the reasons for their retreat to the mainland was shortage of fuel, as over the years they had depleted the scanty turf available to them.

The people who founded Ireland's biggest cities—Dublin, at the head of the bay where the Liffey pours into the sea; Cork, by the Lee, beside one of the biggest natural harbours in Europe; and Limerick, at the upper tidal reaches of the Shannon—were invaders from the sea. The blood of the Norsemen who pillaged monasteries before they settled far from their homes in Scandinavia has mingled with native Celtic stock. An early Gaelic poem written fifteen hundred years ago represents the Irish as a seafaring people. The waters to the southwest of Ireland were the richest fishing grounds in Europe, and in the Middle Ages boats from France and Spain would seek to fish off the coast, paying their dues to chieftains such as O'Sullivan Beare.

Today's trawlers are the final stage of a vigourous seagoing tradition that embraced the currach, the hooker, and the seine boat. Up to recent times, men who lived on the western seaboard were fishermen and farmers equally, and no cottage was without its barrel of salted fish outside the door. One remnant of the past is to be found all over the west and southwest: piers located in a remote place along the coastline. These are the legacy of the Congested Districts Board that functioned around the beginning of the twentieth century to serve the needs of rural places, which were indeed full of people. Emigration has meant that many of the places that benefitted from the board are now silent and empty, with only the strongly made, stout little piers remaining; no doubt they will last as long as the castles and ring forts beside them.

From West Cork, emigrants would go by train to Cobh and take the Cunard and White Star liners, which every Sunday would sail right along the south coast until they passed beyond the Fastnet lighthouse. Those who remained behind would know when the travellers would pass and look out for them; some lit bonfires on the hill so their people could see the smoke from the deck of the ship.

For those who remained there were years of poverty to be endured. Life was hard. "The food I got was hen's eggs, lumps of butter, and bits of fish, limpets and winkles—a bit of everything from sea and land." But there were compensations. Old fishermen reminisce about the fish that filled the sea—the plaice, hake, cod, and bream, every class of fish waiting to be caught on the long line. Above all there was the treasure of the sea, the lobster, still creeping over the floor of every harbour.

At every shift of the pots you would get a dozen lobsters and that meant a dozen shillings; those twelve shillings bought a half sack of flour, and eight shillings a half sack of meal, and so with everything else. A poor man could live easily in those days.

The Blasket islanders used to sell their lobsters to passing French trawlers. The captains would lift up the crustaceans one in each hand, counting "deux... quartre ... six ...huit...." As a result the islanders could count in French in even numbers.

It is fatally easy to fall under the spell of nostalgia and remember the old ways as idyllic. In my lifetime the average farm kept its full compliment of livestock, and bread was cooked in a pot oven over the turf fire. Like the emigrant in London or Boston we tend to remember this seductive picture of old Ireland, where people lived simply and well in beautiful places.

The poverty tends to be forgotten as we come to terms with the changed ideals and ambitions represented by bungalows, second summer homes, yachts, heritage parks with designated views, golf courses, country clubs, and singing pubs and discos. Prosperity and modern farming techniques do little for the picturesque. There must be a place for tourism in modern Ireland. Ireland aspires to be a rich country but is not. "Every poor country accepts tourism as an unavoidable degradation," wrote V. S. Naipaul.

There remains the influence of religion. Christianity may be under attack, but if it is not immutable, it is formidable. Its strength is older than its formal origins. A subtle combination of ancient paganism wedded to the doctrine of the Nazarene continues to give Irish life its greatest force and expression. Holy wells scattered with pennies and medals with scraps of rag tied to the thorn tree above them are found all over the countryside. Their waters welling magically out of the ground were sacred before the coming of Christianity; now, as these waters are taken away in Coke bottles to be placed beside the aspirin, their curative powers are still ascribed to a saint or to the Blessed Virgin. On St. John's Eve the bonfires are lit. The summer months are associated with ancient patterns and pilgrimages many of whose origins are pagan. On Lough Derg in Donegal thousands spend three days making penitential exercises around the small island, which was reputed to contain a secret opening into hell. In the Middle Ages pilgrims came there from all over Europe to perform similar penances.

On the last Sunday in July over forty thousand people climb Croagh Patrick along the ancient "Tochar Phadraig," the pilgrim's way. "The devotees creeping up the side gave an appearance of motion to the whole mountain," noted a nineteenth-century traveller, and it is the same today. This pilgrimage up the stony path of the "lofty almost regular pyramid" must be one of the great spectacles of Europe: a continuous line of people, many in bare feet, others carrying staves, ascending and descending the steep path above Clew bay and its islands. The pilgrims continue all day long, amid shifting clouds and rain broken by shafts of sunlight.

autumn
an fómtar

The first Sunday in August, coinciding with the ancient festival of Lughnasa, was regarded as the end of summer. On Garlic or Lammas Sunday the first potatoes were lifted. "A farmer should have three things on Garlic Sunday—a stack of unthreshed oats, a stack of old turf and a pit of old potatoes." August brought the promise of harvest after the hardship of July, known as the hungry month when all too often the previous year's supplies were exhausted. On the first Sunday of August, Fraughan Sunday was celebrated by picking fraughans (bilberries), which were gathered in rush baskets. The feast marked the end of hunger and the beginning of harvest.

The colours of the August landscape are bright. Fuchsia, a nineteenth-century import from Patagonia, whose bell-shaped purple and scarlet flowers pervade the hedgerows of the west, has run wild in many places. Montbretia, another newcomer, originally from southern Africa, is the result of crossing two species of iris; the hybrid (crocosmia and crocosmiflora), has escaped the garden and is now well established in the moister parts of the country, where its orange trumpets contrast with the native purple loosetrife in the same garish way as the heather and gorse on the mountains.

The white shrubs have gone to berries—first the brilliant orange rowans, followed by the sealing-wax-red hawthorn and the dark purple elderberries. Blackberries ripen:

> At first, just one, a glossy purple clot
> Among others, red, green, hard as a knot.
> You ate that first one and its flesh was sweet,
> Like thickened wine: summer's blood was in it
> Leaving stains upon the tongue and lust for picking.

If the young Seamus Heaney had boiled up his blackberries promptly he would have avoided the "rat-grey fungus" that is the subject for lament in the second part of his poem. Brambles, which are widespread and abundant in woods, hedges, and bushy waste places, vary considerably; over three hundred subspecies have been identified, each with minute differences of berry and of ripening. In the southwest, blackberries are already waiting to be picked at the beginning of August, but near Dublin the small, hard, fruit will not be ready until mid-September at the earliest. They must be picked before Halloween; otherwise the devil will have spat on them.

Black and Tans, Skarteen

It has been said that the word *harvest* is a synonym for autumn. After the hay harvest come barley and wheat and the lifting of the main crop in October. Long before that is the sampling of new potatoes; a childhood memory is the pleasure of tasting new potatoes liberally smeared with country butter. New potatoes, new carrots, strawberries, and raspberries warmed by the sun are memories of summer past. I am old enough to recall stooking sheaves of corn and watching rabbits running for safety as the last patch was cut. Then came the arrival at the farm of the giant threshing machine with its pulleys and innumerable wheels. Men armed with pitchforks, sweat pouring down their faces, fed the machine a cloud of golden rain.

The end of the holidays comes abruptly, with coastal towns emptying overnight. One day the houses and streets are filled with holiday makers, and the next day they are gone. The yachts are lifted out of the water; the fishing season ends. In the old days Michaelmas meant Fomhar na nGean, the goose harvest, when geese hatched in spring were ready for the market. A goose was traditionally eaten on Michaelmas Day. For some the summer is only a tedious interval of waiting before hunting begins. Somerville and Ross caught the mood of October cub hunting:

The alarm clock had shrilled its exulting and age-long summons in the pitchy dark…. I had groped my way through the puddles in the stable yard, and got to my horse by the light of a lantern, and at 5:30 I was over the worst. The meet was nine miles away…. It was still an hour before sunrise, but a pallor was in the sky, and the hounds, that had at first been like a gliding shoal of fish round the horses' feet, began to take on their own shapes and colours.

There are twenty hunts in the country that accept visiting riders willing to pay the "Cap" and face the banks and stone walls. Cubbing, which is largely a test of young hounds, extends to the end of October, when hunting proper begins and the winter is launched.

Every race meeting is a festival as flat racing cedes to the steeplechasing. Racing and hunting still set the social tone, and if you want to be seen as successful, a step that is almost essential is the purchase of a horse. Shows such as the August Show of the Royal Dublin Society and the Horse Show at Millstreet attract international riders. In September the Connemara Pony Show at Clifden shows off the native breed. At the beginning of October the great fair at Ballinasloe, once famous for providing mounts for the British army, is a vivid reminder of the importance of the horse in Irish life.

> Four white feet, send him far away
> Three white feet, keep him for a day
> Two white feet, he may never pay
> One white foot, he is bred to stay.

Ballinasloe was originally a cattle and sheep fair, a centre of routes determined by the natural patterns of esker ridges. Autumn, when livestock had benefitted from summer grazing and harvest, was the time for the big fairs as differentiated from the regular, smaller monthly fairs. In Celtic times Oenacha, or fair assemblies, where kings and nobles attended and religious ceremonies took place, were an annual occurrence. These continued into the Christian era. *The Annals of the Four Masters* describes the Lughnasa fair at Teltown in County Meath in 1168 when the line of horses and carts was six miles long. There are still autumn sheep fairs in mountainous areas such as Wicklow and Donegal, and a few big fairs survive. Puck Fair used to be a Lughnasa fair, but its date has been put back to summer. Lammas Fair in Ballycastle continues a lively tradition. But the monthly fairs have gone; fair day has widely given way to the marts, generally acknowledged to be a more efficient way of disposing of stock than the old tangling and handslapping.

Fruit and berries take on their harvest colours and the bracken turns foxy brown. Hazelnuts, once an important item of the medieval diet, ripen in hedges and copses. The earliest trees to turn gold and yellow are beech and horse chestnut, trees that, although they are well established here, are not actually Irish natives. The beech, which was not introduced until the eighteenth century, has spread widely and successfully, liking the moist conditions it has found here. Beech and horse chestnut, together with the sycamore, came to Ireland from more southerly and warmer lands; they bud earlier in spring and lose their leaves earlier in autumn than other trees. The old natives oak and ash may be descendants of trees that lived in a harsher climate nearer to the Ice Age and kept their leaves until the killing frosts were over. The leaves cling through wind and rain; the splendour of autumn does not touch the oaks until October, when a stand of trees such as those at the Glen of the Downs in County Wicklow or the oak trees of Killarney take on their magnificent

colouring. In recent years our elms have been lost to disease; in many patches of forest their whitened skeletons are still visible, giving a reminder of winter.

The equinoxial storms come out of a clear sky. Around the west coast the waves, usually driven by westerly winds, break against the great cliff formations. At Mizen head, on the extreme southwest of the country, the spray, touched with a rainbow, rises and travels for hundreds of yards over the rough grass above the cliffs. Elsewhere the effect of attacking waves can be even more dramatic when the spray is thrown up to a height of three hundred feet. Some of the western cliffs are immense—two thousand feet high at Slieve League in County Donegal, and higher still at Achill. Waves lash the coast of northern Mayo, one of the most desolate parts of Ireland, flooding into the sea chasm at Moista Sound, pounding the arch at Porturlin and the great line of cliffs running to Benwee head. In comparison, the cliffs of Moher seem almost modest, descending six hundred feet to the water; they are still impressive places to view an autumn storm.

On the east coast of Ireland the effects of wind and rain are less evident on the softer scenery. From Carnsore point to Dublin bay the low eroding cliffs, punctuated by a number of promontories such as Bray head, Wicklow head, and Arklow head, cannot offer the drama of western storms.

The arrival and departure of migrating birds is spread over late summer and autumn. For the casual bird watcher the earliest departure is that of the swift in early August, when almost overnight there is an abrupt cessation of their shrieks above the towns. Swallows will linger until October, raising what is often their third brood; it is debatable how many of these late fledglings can develop enough stamina for the journey south.

From early autumn the winter migrants begin arriving. Waders, such as grey plover, godwits, and dunlin, make their way to estuaries and mudflats having travelled from their summer nesting places in the Arctic. Early in October the geese appear. On the Wexford slobs the V-shaped formations of white-fronted geese fly in from Greenland and settle down for the winter. Until the new year there is enough gleaning for them, but in late winter as their food grows scarce they attack the new crops, and the final rustle and plaintive honking that announce their departure in February are music to the farmer.

Many thousands of these geese winter on the slobs, and Brent geese and Canada geese fly into the marshes at Bull island on the north side of Dublin, on estuaries of the Shannon, and at other locations. The swan seen most generally is the graceful mute swan that is with us all the year round. In summer its huge nest, piled on a mound of water plants and vigorously defended with hisses and snorts, is a familiar sight beside most waterways. On an October evening William Butler Yeats saw nine and fifty swans on the lake at Coole "all suddenly mount and scatter wheeling in great broken rings upon their clamorous wings." In winter two other species of swan, the Bewick and the whooper, fly in, having nested in the Arctic tundra.

Although the numbers of winter migrants remains healthy, they have sadly diminished over the last hundred years. The decrease in bird stocks is a worldwide problem, but it is particularly striking to read accounts of the numbers of water birds in Ireland long ago. They teemed on every lake, river, marsh, bog, and estuary, their numbers in the ten-thousands; every little pond, bog, or marsh had its attendant "bean goose" or greylag to be shot or trapped; on the slobs and the Shannon estuary wild fowlers made a hardy if uncomfortable living. The author of a handbook, *The Fowler in Ireland*, published in 1882, boasted of the fifteen hundred ducks he shot in the winter of 1880. Others did better.

Captain Nugent ... obtained ninety-six wigeon at a shot. Mr. Vincent picked up eighty wigeon and teal after one discharge of his largest gun. He also obtained twenty-six geese at a shot.... In Cork harbour a gentleman fowler was on one occasion forced to throw birds overboard ... to avoid sinking in his single-handed punt.

It is the same with fish. "What splendid angling this wild country offers," wrote William Hamilton Maxwell at the beginning of the nineteenth century. "It spoils one in after life." His *Wild Sports of the West* brought fishermen from England in pursuit of abundant fish. "We landed five salmon besides taking a pannier full of seatrout." The abundance continued well into this century. I talked to a fisherman in western Mayo who remembered the carts coming down to Ballycroy forty years ago to pick up the salmon; sixty fish would be landed with a single cast of the net. In suburban Dublin houses, the maids would threaten to strike if they were offered salmon more than three times a week.

The schedules of the returning seatrout and salmon, and the well-being of trout and coarse fish stocked in our lakes, are easily disturbed. The threats are diverse. Overfishing, salmon farming, sea lice, slurry, and pollution each have their effect on fish stocks. There is a theory that the magical radar that enables a salmon to return to the same river where it spawned has been disrupted because of cross-breeding with farmed fish. How much longer the great rivers and lakes can satisfy fishermen and women is a matter for concern.

And yet in secret places the fish are to be found. Recently, on a limestone lake, a friend hooked a pike with a jaw as long as a shoe; another day he landed a trout that fed six people. There are fish to be caught on the silver grey waters of Lough Mask, Lough Corrib, Lough Carra, and the brown stretches of the Blackwater, the Boyne, the Shannon, and every other fisherman's paradise where the spin of the cast and the plop of rising fish spell happiness.

The fly-fishing season is over now in October and the trout have a reprieve; the angler must rest. Time to reflect on the past year: the first run of the salmon in January, the rise of the mayfly in early summer bringing the dapping season where the trout are tempted with long-legged flies on the end of slender willow dapping rods; the snap and pull of the line signalling a fish on the hook, and the triumphant sweep of the landing net. We can see ourselves as Yeats saw the sun-freckled fisherman in grey Connemara clothes, "climbing up to a place where stone is dark under froth, and the down-turn of his wrist when the flies drop in the stream."

In the past the main potato crop was lifted by the end of October; today mechanization has meant that the half-acre of ridged lazy beds outside each farmhouse is as rarely seen as flocks of hens. The lazy bed or cultivation ridge was misnamed; it was a painstaking method of manuring and improving poor, wet soil and raising its fertility by use of the spade. The Irish spade, the most important of agricultural tools before mechanized farming, had a long straight shaft and bent blade, adapted to turn the sod so that it was a hand plough rather than a digging tool. Although it differed slightly from region to region all over Ireland, it was the perfect tool for the production of the potato. Seamus Heaney remembered his father at work:

> The coarse boot nestled on the lug, the shaft
> Against the inside knee was levered firmly.
> He rooted out tall tops, buried the bright edge deep
> To scatter new potatoes that we picked
> Loving their cool hardness in our hands.
>
> By God, the old man could handle a spade
> Just like his old man.

The potato favours water-retaining soils, which is why, more than any other crop, it flourishes in Ireland. The tragedy that its introduction brought was ironically a result of its virtues. Eaten in sufficient quantities (over six pounds per day), it provides a totally adequate and nutritious diet; for centuries millions of people ate potatoes and water, perhaps seasoned with pepper, and little or nothing else. The potato's introduction has been associated elsewhere—in modern Nepal, for example—with an increase in population. The population in Ireland reached over eight million by the time calamity struck; the fact that so many depended on one crop spelt disaster when the blight-bearing fungus

Phytophthora infestans arrived in Europe from North America. The lazy bed leaves scars in the soil that are as enduring as old ruins. In the west the lines of old fields or the remains of rundale systems can be seen high up on hillsides or right on the edge of cliffs in places that seem far away from human habitation. Even if those who so painstakingly tended these far fields with loy and curved spade were not victims of famine, the remoteness of these places suggests suffering and desperation.

Substitutes for the potato sought during the famine included nettles—people would travel miles to churchyards, where nettles grew thickest. The woods were combed for the fruit of holly, beech, and crabapple, together with the leaves and bark of some trees. Crows, frogs, and hedgehogs baked in clay were eaten; stories persist of dogs and foxes made into soup. Today many fruits of autumn are avoided by those who associate them with famine times. The mushroom, which must be sought for in old pasture that has not been touched by lime and fertilizer, has no place in the country person's diet. Given bright weather following a touch of rain or damp, the wild mushroom can still be gathered by the bucketful. Ironically, the cultivated mushroom has gained its spot in the morning fry, proving that improved communication is changing the national diet. Country stores everywhere sell kiwi fruit and garlic. "Garlic!" a shopkeeper said to me recently. "Twenty years ago we couldn't spell it!"

The end of the farming year was celebrated by the ancient festival of Samhain, the first day of winter, November the first. Much folklore lingers concerning the day before, All Hallow's Eve, puca night and *oíche na sprideanna*, when ghosts and spirits were active and sounds of revelry could be heard from ring forts where fairies held their parties. Halloween is still celebrated with sticky apples and masks, bonfires and children knocking on doors, potatoes mixed with green cabbage and butter to make colcannon, and the ring embedded in the barm brack.

More important, it is the time when crops should all be harvested, livestock returned from its summer grazing, apples picked (the puca, or fairy, would foul fruit picked in November), and hay ricks completed. Potatoes were stored in tapering roof-shaped piles, covered with straw and litter and earthed with shovelfuls of loose earth. Debts were settled up, workers were given their wages, rents were paid, and the hire of the next year's tillage and grazing was arranged.

The many pleasures of autumn include the simple sensuous joy of walking through crisp golden beech leaves in Powerscourt and the sight of leaves changing as the sap fails to rise. A tree is picked clean overnight by wind. There are the low-lying mists associated with lowered temperature, spiders' webs etched in dew, and the smell of bonfires. A particular scent of autumn comes with the drop in temperature and the first frosts. But the truest pleasure of autumn is the farmer's knowledge that the harvest is safely gathered.

WINTER
an Geimhreadh

The second of November is the festival of All Souls, when the dead are remembered and prayed for and the family visits their graves. In the old days the floor would be swept and the fire made up; the family would retire early, leaving the door unlatched, for on that night in the year the souls of the dead could visit their old homes.

The days shorten and the country becomes accustomed to what Mary Lavin described as the curfew of lethargy. Winter melancholy sets in with the early frosts. The philosopher and Irish scholar Arland Ussher wrote, "I believe the Irish mind is imbued with a deep inate disillusionment and disbelief in life that was here before Christianity came to our shores and found such a quick response in our people."

Rain takes hold. In winter it can seem endless, particularly in the west, pouring over the Twelve Pins and the great brown bog of Erris, studded with lakes to Blacksod bay. Above it, the Nephin range in Mayo is the largest area in Ireland without a road—only an ancient track crossing mountain and bog, visible as a scar in the turf. Once it linked Bangor Erris and Newport; drovers made their way to Newport fair. Now it is lonelier than it has ever been, and the country beyond still has some of the atmosphere that the sportsman William Maxwell described as "terra incognita, the wilds of Moy and Erris and the lonely Mullet over which the winds blew and the waves drenched the sands in spray."

Some years ago I made a journey in January on foot tracing the route of O'Sullivan Beare and his followers from Bantry bay to Leitrim. Day after day rain bathed the landscape in a grey cloud; the fields were sodden and silent, with the occasional sound of cattle coughing. Black birds burst out of leafless trees covered in ivy. I remembered Heinrich Böll's visit to Ireland:

"The rain here is absolute, magnificent and frightening. To call this rain bad weather is as inappropriate as to call scorching weather fine weather."

Rain is the mark of our winter, to be endured or ignored. The country person is less bothered with anxiety about the weather than are the urban classes. He or she seldom wears a raincoat or carries an umbrella; a group of men standing on a street corner after Mass while the rain pours down is a common enough sight.

Sooner or later the rain clears. The morning is frosty, and then the sun melts the frost to the sound of horses clattering down a muddy lane and the huntsman's cry. There is more to see as the countryside is pared down. Details become important—smoke blowing from nostrils of cattle, a puddle frozen over, a holly tree, mist plucking at the edge of the mountains, and the sounds of rising wind. The pasture loses its verdure, and the wild places, particularly where the long grass has died, become parched and straw-coloured as if a fire has swept over them; the burnt colour of the turf and the orange lichen on rocks enforce this impression. Now the green of Ireland is the evergreen holly and the ivy shrouding the trees.

"Snow … was falling on every part of the dark central plain, on the treeless hills, falling softly upon the Bog of Allen and further westwards softly falling into the dark mutinous Shannon waves." James Joyce's image of a united Ireland is all the more forceful for its rarity. The odd year happens when the snow falls thickly, the sheep are buried and a gate is stepped over, not climbed. Many of us remember the snows of 1947 and 1962, when much of Ireland was choked and thousands of sheep died.

Dublin

We seldom experience "a Most terrible frost and Snow" like that which took place in 1783 and was described by Dorothea Herbert.

The Snow soon became Mountainous high with consequent Inundations that … prevented Man or Beast from stirring—Many Cottages were totally buried in the Snow or demolished by floods.… The Trees were one Sheet of christalized Snow.… We sat the whole time wrapt up in Great Coats over the fire.… We spent the Whole 47 Days while the cold lasted playing Cards and roasting Sprats … [which were] driven in in such plenty that heaps were thrown out every where.

At most other times snow is a sprinkling, a day's wonder that will melt away, although it may linger on the big mountains, firming the outlines of Galtymor or Mount Leinster or the Macgillicuddy Reeks.

In general, winter weather is soft and sodden more often than sharp and frosty. It is a damp cold that pervades bones and gives us rheumatism. It destroys timber and wattle so that in Ireland there is no legacy of black-and-white medieval timber houses as there is in England. Damp and rot had destroyed such houses by the nineteenth century. The incidence of crippling arthritis is high in Ireland, and our surgeons are adept at hip replacement operations. This was the cold that the hermits sought in their freezing cells for penance and self-punishment: "The blessed Ciaran took up his habitation like a hermit in the waste, for all about him was a waste of tangled woodland. He began to build his little cell of mean stuff, and that was the beginning of the monastery." Many ascetics longed for "a cold fearsome bed where one rests like a doomed man." In winter mad Sweeny, Buile Suibhne, was "tormented by frost, falling from the tops of withered branches … walking through furze."

The cold pervades houses; my generation was brought up on the theory of open windows and draughts and the concept that any modern form of heating was wasteful and undesirable. During the long winter evenings we wrapped in rugs and huddled over open fires. Seamus Heaney commemorates the weather forecast and gale warnings:

> Dogger, Rockall, Malin, Irish sea:
> Green, swift upsurges, North Atlantic flux
> Conjured by that strong gale-warning voice
> Collapse into a sibilant penumbra.

Storms and drownings ruled the lives of the Aran islanders encountered by John Synge. An old man told him: "A man who is not afraid of the sea will soon be drowned … for he will be going out on a day he shouldn't. But we do be afraid of the sea, and we do only be drowned now and again."

One of the incidents the playwright witnessed was incorporated in *Riders to the Sea.*

The sister of the dead man … pieced together all she could remember about his clothes, and what his purse was like, and where he had got it, and the same for his tobacco box, and his stockings. In the end there seemed little doubt that it was her brother. "Ah!" she said, "it's Mike sure enough, and please God they'll give him a decent burial."

Storms lash the coast all the year round; a summer storm sank the Armada. In recent times an August gale brought a wind from the south that drowned sixteen yachtsmen in the Fastnet race. Richard Murphy has passed on an unforgettable image of a drowning in a summer storm.

> The woman came from the forecastle
> she came up alone on deck
> and a great heave cast her out on shore
>
> And another heave came while she drowned
> and put her on her knees
> like a person'd be in prayer
>
> That's the way the people found her
> and the sea never came in
> near that mark no more.

But storms are particularly associated with winter, and the annals are full of tales about them. The worst storm within historical memory was perhaps that of February 1839, known as the Big Wind. Herrings were blown through the air like birds. All over the country cabins had their thatch lifted as if by the hand of a giant child seeking to peer into a doll's house; the turf fires of many cottages were blown so that the cottages caught on fire. Next day, in the middle of Ireland, the twigs on every bush tasted of salt. J. M. Callwell, whose childhood was spent in Ross House west of Galway, remembered that "though our old home stands some fifteen miles from the Atlantic as the crow flies, with a range of high hills intervening, the floor of our bedroom in the morning was coated with salt and strewn with seaweed."

Richard Murphy wrote of the Cleggan disaster in 1929 that destroyed a community:

> Lanterns shafted from the gates of the fish-store
> Freshly that night cleaned for a ceili.
> Bodies of fishermen lay on the floor on boxes
> Blood on their faces. Five had been found
> By troops of searchers on shingle and sand.
> Over the bier, with one hand cupping a flame,
> An old man was looking at his drowned son.
> Of those who survived, a young one was seen
> Walking at noon in the fields, clutching a bailer.

Winter, when the tourists have gone, is the time for seeing ruins and antiquities, castles outlined against sharp light, the smothered remains of a country house, a passage grave, a ring fort, or a ring of stones or alignments of stones such as the Three Fingers at Castletownshend in Cork or Finn Macool's Fingers in Cavan. A lonely place on a January day is enhanced by the effects of cold and perhaps by a harsh wind or lemon-yellow afternoon light or a blood-red setting sun. This is the time to stop by a castle wall—perhaps at the Lacey castle at Trim, the huge fortress at Liscarroll, or the ruin of a house such as Burntcourt in Tipperary or Moore Hall on Lough Carra. The abbeys and friarys—Cisterian, Franciscan Jerpoint, Kilconnel, Mellifont, Timoleague and the rest—are given the pleasure of discovery in a season when visitors are scarce. Winter is time to seek out unforgettable places such as the roofless remains of Rosserk beside the dark waters of the Moy estuary, or the vast, mysterious semicircle of the fort of Dun Aengus on Aran Mor backing against a cliff, with waves pounding hundreds of feet below.

The remains of one of Ireland's greatest archeological sites are at their most dramatic in the winter months. The megalithic cemetery at Loughcrew in County Meath is situated on the ridge that encompasses Slieve na Calliagh, the Hag's mountain, Patrick's Town, and Carnbane West. A ring fort tumuli, pillar stones, and chambered cairns lie in scattered glory all over these rounded hills that look down over a wide, enduring landscape bounded by Lough Sheelin.

At midwinter, prehistoric humans timed very precisely the moment when the days would start lengthening, and in many places the timepieces that marked the period, when sun struck sacred stone, are still to be found. The most impressive of these is the huge mound at Newgrange, a cairn a hundred yards across and forty feet high, whose covering of white quartz stones has been painstakingly restored. With the aid of a permit from the Board of Works, a few privileged spectators over the period of the winter solstice are permitted into the inner chamber at dawn, where the beam from the rising sun trickles up the passage like running water.

But although Newgrange is one of the most impressive ruins in Europe, the archeologists have restored and tidied it up so that it has about as much atmosphere as an airport. Prehistoric inhabitants also coaxed the sun to rise in lesser places, where it still appears at a formal moment, even if it has shifted a little in the thousands of years since the original alignment was made. Some of these places have taken on new layers of legend, such as Piper's Stones in Wicklow, where the ring and the stone outside represent the piper and dancers punished for revelry on a holy day. In many other solitary locations, often on a sloping hillside, stone circles are slanted to catch the sun at dawn as it makes the first movement toward a renewed year. At Drumbeg and Dunbeacon in Cork, Athgreany and Ballyfolan in Wicklow, Ballynoe in County Down and elsewhere, stones were set in circles to mark the end of winter.

Christmas, originally associated with the winter solstice, was thoroughly Christianized. It was the most important festival in the year, requiring spiritual preparation in the form of fasting all Advent. The house was cleaned and hung with holly, ivy, bay, and laurel. Poitín was laid in for hospitality. On Christmas morning after Mass, women prepared the goose or beef while men played games, often hurley, or hunted hares. While leaving the church after Mass some people took wisps of straw from the crib for winter's luck.

The day after Christmas used to be notable for the Wren boys going around with their little corpse. There must have been a sense of the barbaric at the sight of young men in their mummer's clothes processing from door to door with their holly branch decorated with ribbons and a stiff, dead bird beaten out of a bush. Folklorists are sheepish about this macabre custom, once widespread and accepted without protest or comment; its origins are unknown, although it seems probable that it forms part of some remnant of a sacrificial ceremony.

New year's—not a festival of importance in rural Ireland—followed by the lengthening days, points the way to the true new year and the first day of spring, with Brighid as its sponsor. The year has brought its different aspects to the island of Ireland, now wrapped in winter. Ireland's landscape has its delights at every moment of the year. It would be pleasant to believe that the mountains and hills, the bogs and the rich green fields, will retain their beauty for centuries—for at least as long again as the ring forts and round towers have been landmarks. But the country is under threat.

Frank Mitchell has written, "The landscape will continue to deteriorate unless the Irish people will put aside the golden calf, and turn again to the husbandry of the Four Green Fields." In winter one thinks of these things: uncontrolled ribbon development, a bungalow built beside a beauty spot, hedges torn up, heather-covered mountains smothered in sombre fir trees, pollution of our lakes, Georgian buildings gone to ruin, and all the other signs of destruction. It may be prejudice to think that in Ireland we have more to lose than elsewhere, but Tom Kelly's photographs testify that this indeed is the case.

sea

an mhuir

West Cork coastline

SHORELINE

Turning a corner, taking a hill
In County Down, there's the sea
Sidling and settling to
The back of a hedge. Or else

A grey bottom with puddles
Dead-eyed as fish.
Haphazard tidal craters march
The corn and the grazing.

All round Antrim and westward
Two hundred miles at Moher
Basalt stands to,
Both ocean and channel

Froth at the black locks
On Ireland. And strands
Take hissing submissions
Off Wicklow and Mayo.

Take any minute. A tide
Is rummaging in
At the foot of all fields,
All cliffs and shingles.

Listen. Is it the Danes,
A black hawk bent on the sail?
Or the chinking Normans?
Or currachs hopping high

On to the sand?
Strangford, Arklow, Carrickfergus,
Belmullet and Ventry
Stay, forgotten like sentries.

Mayo coastline

Atlantic coast, County Clare

Lough Swilly, County Donegal

Dunmanus Bay, West Cork

Sliabh League, County Donegal

Atlantic coast, County Clare

The Skelligs, County Kerry

Achill Island, County Mayo

Inishtooskert, County Kerry

Dublin Bay

Donegal Bay

55

Land

faoin tuath

Dunmanus Bay, West Cork

Three Castle Head, West Cork

Cliffs of Moher, County Clare

Gouganebarra, County Cork

Cape Clear Island, County Cork

63

Wicklow

Mizen Head, West Cork

BOGLAND

for T. P. Flanagan

We have no prairies
To slice a big sun at evening—
Everywhere the eye concedes to
Encroaching horizon,

Is wooed into the cyclops' eye
Of a tarn. Our unfenced country
Is bog that keeps crusting
Between the sights of the sun.

They've taken the skeleton
Of the Great Irish Elk
Out of the peat, set it up
An astounding crate full of air.

Butter sunk under
More than a hundred years
Was recovered salty and white.
The ground itself is kind, black butter

Melting and opening underfoot,
Missing its last definition
By millions of years.
They'll never dig coal here,

Only the waterlogged trunks
Of great firs, soft as pulp.
Our pioneers keep striking
Inwards and downwards,

Every layer they strip
Seems camped on before.
The bogholes might be Atlantic seepage.
The wet centre is bottomless.

Wicklow Mountains

Croagh Patrick, County Mayo

Killarney, County Kerry

Wicklow Mountains

Croagh Patrick, County Mayo

County Kerry

Nephin, County Mayo

Castlebar, County Mayo

plants

na planndaí

The Glen, County Sligo

Forest, County Wicklow

May bush and well, County Offaly

Rape field, east coast

Schull, West Cork

Mizen Head, West Cork

Bloody Crane's Bill, Burren, County Clare

Black Head, Burren, County Clare

West Cork

Wild primroses

Bog cotton, Sneem, County Kerry

Crit Island, County Donegal

87

Classie Bawn, County Sligo

Dunkelly, West Cork

THE PLANTATION

Any point in that wood
Was a centre, birch trunks
Ghosting your bearings
Improvising charmed rings

Wherever you stopped.
Though you walked a straight line
It might be a circle you travelled
With toadstools and stumps

Always repeating themselves.
Or did you re-pass them?
Here were bleyberries quilting the floor,
The black char of a fire

And having found them once
You were sure to find them again.
Someone had always been there
Though always you were alone.

Lovers, birdwatchers,
Campers, gipsies and tramps
Left some trace of their trades
Or their excrement.

Hedging the road so
It invited all comers
To the hush and the mush
Of its whispering treadmill,

Its limits defined,
So they thought, from outside.
They must have been thankful
For the hum of the traffic

If they ventured in
Past the picnickers' belt
Or began to recall
Tales of fog on the mountains.

You had to come back
To learn how to lose yourself,
To be pilot and stray—witch,
Hansel and Gretel in one.

County Tipperary

LIVING

an saol

Turf gathering, County Kerry

95

Gallarus Oratory, County Kerry

Midlands farmer

Ballinasloe Horse Fair market

Ennis, County Clare

Diviner, County Meath

THE DIVINER

Cut from the green hedge a forked hazel stick
That he held tight by the arms of the V:
Circling the terrain, hunting the pluck
Of water, nervous, but professionally

Unfussed. The pluck came sharp as a sting.
The rod jerked down with precise convulsions,
Spring water suddenly broadcasting
Through a green aerial its secret stations.

The bystanders would ask to have a try.
He handed them the rod without a word.
It lay dead in their grasp till nonchalantly
He gripped expectant wrists. The hazel stirred.

Session, Westport, County Mayo

Skibbereen, County Cork

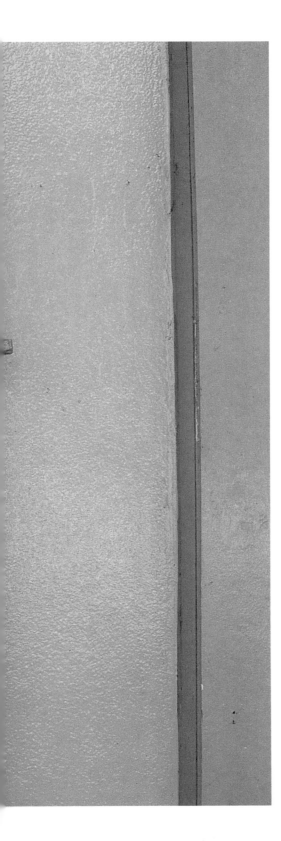

Eyeries, County Cork

Ballinasloe Horse Fair

Horses, County Kildare

Trout, County Galway

Killeen Castle, County Meath

Cliffs of Moher, County Clare

Galway / Mayo border

County Mayo

Glenheist, County Mayo

115

stone

clochach

CAIRN-MAKER

For Barrie Cooke

He robbed the stones' nests, uncradled
As he orphaned and betrothed rock
To rock: his unaccustomed hand
Went chambering upon hillock

And bogland. Clamping, balancing,
That whole day spent in the Burren,
He did not find and add to them
But piled up small cairn after cairn

And dressed some stones with his own mark.
Which he tells of with almost fear;
And of strange affiliation
To what was touched and handled there,

Unexpected hives and castlings
Pennanted now, claimed by no hand:
Rush and ladysmock, heather-bells
Blowing in each aftermath of wind.

Poulnabroine, County Clare

Stone circle, Lough Crew, Counties Meath and Cavan

Lough Crew

Burial chamber and stone circle, Lough Crew

West Cork

West Cork

Limestone, County Clare

Hungry Hill, West Cork

Tara, County Meath

Clifden, County Galway

Dunmoe Castle, County Meath

Corcomroe Abbey, County Clare

water

uisce

Glendalough, County Wicklow

136

WATERFALL

The burn drowns steadily in its own downpour,
A helter-skelter of muslin and glass
That skids to a halt, crashing up suds.

Simultaneous acceleration
And sudden braking; water goes over
Like villains dropped screaming to justice.

It appears an athletic glacier
Has reared into reverse: is swallowed up
And regurgitated through this long throat.

My eye rides over and downwards, falls with
Hurtling tons that slabber and spill,
Falls, yet records the tumult thus standing still.

Glendalough, County Wicklow

County Donegal

County Mayo

Wexford Slobs, County Wexford

Swan, County Waterford

River Liffey, Dublin

Lough Meelagh, County Roscommon

Killary Harbour, County Mayo

Galway Bay

County Limerick

Delphi, County Mayo

Dublin Mountains

Finlough, Delphi, County Mayo

Connemara, County Galway

sky

an spéir

Wicklow Mountains

Ben Bulben, County Sligo

County Sligo

Connemara, Galway

Lough Ennell, Westmeath

Twelve Pins, Connemara, County Galway

160

Donegal coast

Sligo Mountains and Donegal Bay

Connemara, County Galway

Trim, County Meath

Clonmacnoise on the Shannon

Bective Abbey, County Meath

County Waterford

Blasket Islands, County Kerry

GOOD-NIGHT

A latch lifting, an edged den of light
Opens across the yard. Out of the low door
They stoop into the honeyed corridor,
Then walk straight through the wall of the dark.

A puddle, cobble-stones, jambs and doorstep
Are set steady in a block of brightness.
Till she strides in again beyond her shadows
And cancels everything behind her.

County Meath